# ActionBarSherlock

## Implementing Support on Older Android Versions

# Table of Contents

# Chapter 1. Introduction

Diving into the ever-evolving world of Android app development, our Special Report navigates a highly crucial but often overlooked topic: ActionBarSherlock. Offering a comprehensive analysis, this report uncovers the compelling subject of implementing ActionBarSherlock Support on Older Android Versions. Preempting the hurdles designers and developers may face due to operating system diversifications, this study demystifies the process of retroactive compatibility on Android. Offering insights and clarifications, it unpacks complex technicalities with a grounded, accessible approach. This special report is designed to arm you with the needed tactical knowledge to broaden your app's user base, embrace inclusivity by supporting legacy platforms, and ultimately turbocharge your success in the bustling Android app marketplace. No jargon-heavy technobabble here – we tackle these software hurdles in a way that even your grandma would understand!

# Chapter 2. Understanding ActionBarSherlock: A Primer

ActionBarSherlock is a widely acclaimed library that was developed to allow backward compatibility with older versions of Android. This primer on ActionBarSherlock delves into the multifaceted nature of the library, explaining what it is, how it works, and the benefits of incorporating it into our own applications.

A deep-rooted understanding of ActionBarSherlock will empower developers to create apps that are aesthetic, functional, and inclusive of a wider range of Android versions.

## 2.1. Defining ActionBarSherlock

ActionBarSherlock, originally developed by Jake Wharton, is an extension of the support library designed to facilitate the use of the ActionBar design pattern across varying versions of Android with a smooth, seamless implementation. It allows developers to use a consistent API while crafting their applications by providing backward compatibility as far as Android 2.x. The ActionBar pattern itself is an integral component of the Android user interface that provides control, navigation, and other options within easy reach for users.

## 2.2. Unlocking ActionBarSherlock Capabilities

ActionBarSherlock is laced with a host of features and capabilities. These include overarching, system-level control elements such as action buttons, navigations modes, and more:

1. **Action Items**: Buttons located in the action bar used for

frequently accessed functionalities.

2. **Navigation Modes**: Various modes such as tab navigation and dropdown navigation to aid seamless user movement within an application.

3. **Overflow**: The 'more' section of the action bar that houses secondary functionalities and actions.

With ActionBarSherlock, developers can implement these user interface elements with ease, and maintain a consistent experience across different Android versions.

## 2.3. The Importance of ActionBarSherlock

While Android's advancements in recent years have obviated the necessity of ActionBarSherlock for the newer versions, there remains a significant proportion of devices running older Android versions worldwide. Using ActionBarSherlock in your application development process ensures that you do not alienate this segment of your potential user base and allows your apps to reach a wider audience.

In addition, learning ActionBarSherlock stands as an exciting and transformative journey for developers looking to sharpen their skills and tap into the full power of Android programming.

## 2.4. Integrating ActionBarSherlock into Android Studio

To start using ActionBarSherlock, you need to integrate it into your Android Studio environment. You can download the library from the official GitHub page and import it as a module. Once imported, you can add it to your application by extending SherlockActivity or other such base classes provided by the library. This will enable your application to access features and implement the ActionBar in your app.

# 2.5. Deep Dive: ActionBarSherlock Components

The ActionBarSherlock library comes with several crucial components that enhance user experience and make navigation within the app a delight. These components include:

1. **ActionBar.Tab**: This is a component representing each tab in the ActionBarSherlock.

2. **ActionBar.LayoutParams**: This set of layout parameters augments the human-machine interaction in the app by specifying how elements in the ActionBar are placed.

3. **ActionBarSherlock.OnMenuVisibilityListener**: This interface allows response to changes in the visibility of the action bar.

Understanding these components and their interactions forms the crux of ActionBarSherlock operation.

In conclusion, ActionBarSherlock remains a pivotal tool in Android app development, permitting app compatibility across multiple Android versions. Full understanding and proper usage of ActionBarSherlock, therefore, stands as a prerequisite for becoming a proficient, successful, and inclusive Android developer.

# Chapter 3. Diving Deep into Android Versions

Before we delve into ActionBarSherlock, it is crucial to visit the landscape of Android versions. A heterogeneous range of Android versions are in use globally, and it becomes essential for an application to support older versions to reach the widest audience possible.

## 3.1. Understanding Android Versions: A Brief History

Android, introduced to the world in 2007, has seen several editions since its inception. Operating system (OS) upgrades are a routine part of technology progression and Android is no exception.

From the initial version, Android 1.0, to the current latest, Android 12, every iteration has added critical new features while revising existing ones. Different Android versions are recognized by their unique codenames, most of them named in alphabetical order after a dessert, from Cupcake (1.5) to Pie (9.0). Starting with Android 10, a simple numeric naming system was adopted.

## 3.2. User Diversity and Android Versions

By supporting older Android versions, developers can leverage the user base. According to StatCounter, as of 2020, no single Android version holds more than 20% of the global market share. The various Android versions display a distributed and diverse user base. This diversity necessitates a robust strategy to ensure apps remain accessible to users with older devices.

# 3.3. The ActionBarSherlock Influence in Versions

Since Android 3.0, Google introduced ActionBar, a critical part of delivering an effective user interface. However, older versions had difficulties in supporting ActionBar, leading to the introduction of ActionBarSherlock.

ActionBarSherlock ensured compatibility for Android versions as early as 2.x. It filled the gap by providing a similar ActionBar experience for older versions, helping developers maintain the consistency of their apps.

# 3.4. Challenges in Version Support

Supporting older versions comes with its unique set of challenges. Some hurdles include:

1. Decreased performance and speed: Older versions may lag with certain functionality, affecting the overall user experience. Developers must be careful not to overload these versions.

2. Different user interface: The aesthetic and functional aspects of Android have advanced significantly over the years. Adapting these changes for older versions requires thought and effort.

3. Testing and debugging: Ensuring the app performs seamlessly across all versions demands rigorous testing and can often lead to challenging debugging sessions.

# 3.5. Strategies to Encourage Backward Compatibility

Several methodologies can help simplify supporting older Android versions.

1. Using Compatibility Libraries: Android Compatibility library and ActionBarSherlock are examples of these. They help developers use modern APIs on older versions.

2. Performance management: Developers must ensure that sophisticated functionalities do not overload older versions. Having a version-specific user interface helps to manage this.

3. Lower API Levels: Setting a lower minimum SDK version in the app specification helps the app to reach more users. However, this choice requires a balance between more coverage and potential performance issues.

4. Testing: Virtual and physical devices running older versions are used for testing to ensure smooth working.

In conclusion, the importance of backward compatibility for Android apps cannot be overstated. By offering support for older Android versions through libraries like ActionBarSherlock, developers broaden their user base which, in turn, increases their apps' success rates. The task might seem daunting, but with a strategic approach, it is entirely feasible to master this challenge and unlock untapped opportunities.

# Chapter 4. The Importance of Backward Compatibility

While embarking on app development projects, it is crucial to consider the diverse Android landscape. Android proudly wears the hat of the most popular smartphone operating system on the planet, not just because of its user-friendly interface, but primarily for its ubiquity. The Android ecosystem is not a homogenous environment; it's a melting pot of countless devices running different versions of the Android operating system. By ensuring backward compatibility, developers can tap into this expansive user base and substantially expand their app's reach.

## 4.1. Extending Your User Base

One cannot overstate the importance of backward compatibility in richening a developer's landscape. A significant percentage of Android devices are still running old versions of the operating system. Providing support for these versions means that your application could be downloaded and used by users running older Android systems, extending beyond the user base of only the latest Android versions. If you only target newer versions of Android, you might end up alienating a vast user base who are unable or unwilling to upgrade their systems.

## 4.2. Embracing Inclusivity

The beauty of the Android system lies in its diversity. Unlike other operating systems, Android is designed to work on a vast array of hardware, from high-end devices from giants like Samsung and Google to low-cost handsets in developing markets. These affordable devices seldom receive system updates, but they substantially contribute to the fabric of Android's user base. Backward compatibility essentially widens the audience, making your app inclusive and accessible to the greater population rather than a handful of privileged few with access to the recent versions.

# 4.3. Lifecycle Management and Maintenance

An important aspect of app development is lifecycle management. Developing for the lowest possible Android version that your app can support helps with maintenance. When you later decide to support new features brought in by the newer Android versions, you can keep your original code base and add these features as enhancements. This reduces the complexity of your project, helping to ensure smoother progress in the upgrade cycle, and easier maintenance down the line.

# 4.4. Extending App Lifespan

Backward compatibility not only extends your user base but also extends your app's lifespan. Pursuing backward compatibility ensures your app remains relevant and sustainable as newer versions of Android come out. As a result, your users won't need to part ways with your app just because they have not updated their system. Instead, they get to enjoy using your application for longer, thereby enhancing their user experience and fostering brand loyalty.

# 4.5. Inspiring Customer Confidence

In many ways, prioritizing the backward compatibility engenders consumer confidence in your app. When users see that the app runs smoothly on their device, irrespective of its operating system version, they perceive the application and the brand behind it as reliable. This positive user experience boosts user retention and induces new users to download the app, given its broad compatibility and user-friendly operational capacity.

# 4.6. Conclusion

While ensuring backward compatibility might require extra work, it deftly positions your app to span a broader audience and foster more significant market penetration. This strategy invites a higher number of downloads, better rankings on the app store, and potentially more revenue. It's a crucial factor for any developer looking to achieve success in the ever-competitive Android app marketplace.

Remember that every user counts when you aim for a notable presence in the app space. Providing support for different Android versions uplifts your app usability, fostering higher inclusivity. As an Android developer, your mantra should always be 'Leave no user behind.' Backward compatibility enables you to do just that by enhancing your app's accessibility, adaptability, and longevity, thereby setting the stage for unrivaled success.

# Chapter 5. Configuring ActionBarSherlock for Legacy Android

Before diving into configuration, it's useful to start with a brief overview of what ActionBarSherlock is and why it's valuable. With thousands of different Android devices, compatibility is a major concern for app developers. ActionBarSherlock is a library which makes modern Android user experience interfaces, such as the ActionBar, available on older versions of Android (2.x). The ActionBar is a crucial navigational tool, adding visual complexity and function to an app. By tying together a plethora of variables - from diverse screen sizes to differing Android versions - ActionBarSherlock aids in bridging such gaps and ensures broad market inclusion and thus increased potential reach.

## 5.1. Download ActionBarSherlock

As with any external library, the journey to implementing ActionBarSherlock begins with downloading the software itself. Available for free, ActionBarSherlock can be downloaded from the GitHub repository. The process is straightforward: go to the ActionBarSherlock page on Github, and click on the green 'Code' button. For the sake of this guide, select 'Download ZIP' to save the file to your local workstation.

Once downloaded, extract the ZIP file. The resulting folder serves as ActionBarSherlock's library project. Keep this location handy, as it will be important in the later steps of configuration.

# 5.2. Incorporating ActionBarSherlock into your Android Project

To bring ActionBarSherlock into your project's sphere, the Android application project and the ActionBarSherlock library project need to be linked. Open your Android IDE (if you're using an older version of Android Studio, you might need Eclipse).

In the IDE, select 'File > New > Import Project', then navigate to the ActionBarSherlock library project directory. Having imported ActionBarSherlock successfully, now link it to your Android project.

To do this, right-click on your project and follow these steps:

- Select 'Properties'.

- In the Properties window, select 'Android'.

- Under the Library section, click on the 'Add' button.

- From the list that pops up, choose 'ActionBarSherlock' and press 'Ok'.

Double-check that ActionBarSherlock is listed under the libraries with a green tick mark, signifying a successful linking. It's worth mentioning, ActionBarSherlock is dependent on Android 4.0, depicted as API Level 14. This should be marked as the project target in the Android manifest file.

# 5.3. Configuring ActionBarSherlock in Code

Having woven the ActionBarSherlock library into your application project fabric, it's time to utilise it within the code.

Let's start by discussing how to construct your activities so they tie into the ActionBarSherlock functionalities. Activities need to extend either SherlockActivity, SherlockListActivity, or SherlockFragmentActivity. This ensures integration with Android's ActionBar features. As a shard of foresighted advice, remember to replace calls to getActionBar() with getSupportActionBar().

Here's a quick example of how standard Activity configuration would look:

```java
public class MainActivity extends SherlockActivity {
    @Override
    public void onCreate(Bundle savedInstanceState) {
        super.onCreate(savedInstanceState);
        setContentView(R.layout.activity_main);

        ActionBar actionBar = getSupportActionBar();
        actionBar.setDisplayHomeAsUpEnabled(true);
    }
}
```

# 5.4. Customising ActionBarSherlock

Customisation is a key feature of ActionBarSherlock. Not only can you add traditional items - like icons and text - but ActionBarSherlock supports custom navigation modes as well. This includes tabs and drop-down lists.

To implement a custom action bar, it is necessary to first obtain an instance of the ActionBar through the getSupportActionBar() method. With the returned ActionBar object, you can now enable modifications and insert additional functionalities.

Let's have a look at an example of enabling the 'Up' navigation:

```
ActionBar actionBar = getSupportActionBar();
actionBar.setDisplayHomeAsUpEnabled(true);
```

By calling the setDisplayHomeAsUpEnabled method with a value of 'true', the 'Up' navigational carrot is enabled.

ActionBarSherlock extends its flexibility through styles and themes too. By applying the right theme, you can create a unique aesthetic essence suiting your app's spirit. ActionBarSherlock brings with it inbuilt themes designed to be used with the older devices while providing the consistent graphic standard of modern Android.

# 5.5. Conclusion

ActionBarSherlock, with its ability to make newest features available for older versions, is indeed an asset for any Android developer. This guide has ventured to elucidate the process of integrating ActionBarSherlock with a lucid, detailed, and exhaustive approach. With this knowledge, you stand prepared to make your app accomodating, feature-rich, and engaging - even for devices operating on an older Android version. As developers, it is this inclusivity that spells a greater reach and dictates the successful stride in the bustling Android marketplace.

# Chapter 6. Troubleshooting Common ActionBarSherlock Issues

There exist a number of common issues that developers may encounter when implementing ActionBarSherlock, and understanding these issues and their solutions is a vital step in the troubleshooting process. This section will illustrate several of these problems, demonstrating various ways to address them and highlighting the strategies that are known to be most effective.

## 6.1. Updating to the Latest Library Version

As a first step, ensure that you're working with the latest version of ActionBarSherlock. Like any active open-source project, ActionBarSherlock is continually receiving updates that address potential problems and improve its reliability and efficiency. Updating the library isn't always smooth sailing, however. Should you bump into problems after updating, consider the following steps:

1. **Cleaning your project**: This is a good practice whenever you update a library. Under the "Project" menu in Android Studio, click on "Clean project". This also applies if you're using Eclipse; find this option there under the "Project" menu as well.

2. **Checking dependencies**: Newer versions of ActionBarSherlock may entail updated dependencies. Be sure to review the documentation for any changes and adjust your project accordingly.

3. **Confirming compatibility**: Your project's compatibility with the updated version could be suspect. If issues persist after cleaning

your project and verifying your dependencies, some further research or assistance from the development community may be needed.

# 6.2. Dealing with "NoClassDefFoundError"

When ActionBarSherlock is not properly implemented, you might face an issue known as NoClassDefFoundError, a common problem some developers encounter when first using this library.

1. **Check library references**: Be sure ActionBarSherlock is correctly referenced as a library in your project. Double-check your settings and verify that the library is accurately linked to your project.

2. **Use a fully qualified name**: In your XML layout files, you need to use a fully qualified name for custom views. For example, use "com.actionbarsherlock.view.MenuInflater" rather than just "MenuInflater".

3. **Clean and rebuild**: Rebuilding the project after performing these checks can often help resolve this error.

# 6.3. Incompatible Themes

ActionBarSherlock provides a vast collection of styles that can be applied across different app themes. But, in attempting to create a harmonious blend of the old and the new, you can inadvertently generate style conflicts.

Here's how you can avoid them:

1. **Stick to ActionBarSherlock's Themes**: When dealing with ActionBarSherlock, always apply one of its default styles. For example, `Theme.Sherlock,` `Theme.Sherlock.Light,`

`Theme.Sherlock.Light.DarkActionBar` tend to work reliably without conflict.

2. **Avoid mixing App themes**: Given their intricate complexities, stay away from combining components of `App.Theme` with those of ActionBarSherlock's theme. This can lead to clashing attributes and present issues while rendering different controls, which may appear unsightly and inconsistent.

3. **Inspect your theme hierarchies**: A common mistake is not inspecting your theme inheritance. This can lead to using a theme that, at some point in its hierarchy, conflicts with ActionBarSherlock style attributes. Review your themes to ensure harmonious inheritance.

# 6.4. Troubleshooting Menu Items

Menu items not presenting correctly is another common issue in ActionBarSherlock. It can take different forms: an overflow menu item not displaying in the action bar, a custom view not showing up or certain items missing. Here's what you can do:

1. **Check your XML Menu Definitions**: IsValidating your XML menu definitions is necessary. For example, with the attribute `android:showAsAction` consider also using its ActionBarSherlock version `showAsAction`.

2. **Ensure Backwards Compatibility**: When working with ActionBarSherlock, ensure you utilize its API for interacting with the menu. This involves using Sherlock versions of classes such as `SherlockActivity` or `SherlockFragment`.

Conclusion

The road to perfectly retrofitted ActionBarSherlock on older Android versions can be fraught with hurdles, but with the actionable insights presented above, you're now well-equipped to troubleshoot and prevail. Do keep in mind that ActionBarSherlock, like any tool, it is not magical but requires a keen understanding and skillful application. The challenges we've explored here don't represent an exhaustive list but they do provide an excellent starting point in mastering ActionBarSherlock and ensuring smoother implementation of retroactive compatibility on Android.

# Chapter 7. Customizing ActionBarSherlock for an Enhanced User Interface

To fully leverage ActionBarSherlock, it's crucial to comprehend how to customize it. It's not just about functional compatibility with older Android versions but also about creating an enhanced user-interface experience. When your app looks good and feels intuitive across multiple Android versions, it's bound to catch the attention of a larger audience.

## 7.1. Getting Started

First things first, setting up ActionBarSherlock requires the inclusion of the library into your Android project. You can do this by downloading the ActionBarSherlock library, then importing it into your project. Subsequent to the integration, it will be available for use within your app.

Please make sure to update the AndroidManifest.xml file with android:theme="@style/Theme.Sherlock" for each activity that you want to incorporate the ActionBarSherlock in, or just update the application tag if you want it to apply to the entire app.

## 7.2. Customizing ActionBarSherlock

Once ActionBarSherlock is integrated into your app, you can then begin the customization process. The ActionBarSherlock is highly customizable - you can change its background color, adjust its height, add custom views, and much more. Here's a step-by-step approach:

1. **Set to a custom theme**: To set a custom theme for

ActionBarSherlock, create a new style in the styles.xml file complete with the CustomActionBarTheme. This allows you to override the default ActionBarSherlock styles individually. Look for the item named "actionBarStyle" and set your custom style to it.

2. **Change the background color**: Adjusting the ActionBarSherlock's background color can enhance the look and feel of your app. This can be achieved by adding the item "background" to your custom style.

3. **Modify the height**: Want to make your ActionBarSherlock more prominent or more spacious? Try changing its height. Use the item "height" inside your custom style and set its value to your preferred dimension.

4. **Integrate custom views**: ActionBarSherlock supports the addition of custom views. This feature allows you to add controls like buttons, labels, or images to your ActionBarSherlock directly.

# 7.3. Implementing Action Items

Action items are buttons within ActionBarSherlock that perform specific tasks. They help in improving UI interactivity and helps users navigate through your app efficiently. You can add action items by inflating a menu in your SherlockActivity or SherlockFragmentActivity.

Defining these items involves creating a new XML file in the menu directory, where each item represents an action item with a unique id, icon, and title. The item's 'showAsAction' property helps determine if the item should be displayed as a button in the ActionBarSherlock or in the drop-down overflow menu.

# 7.4. Working with Tab Navigation

ActionBarSherlock also enables you to take advantage of tab navigation - a commonly implemented UI model across many Android apps. You can add tabs to your ActionBarSherlock, and use these to navigate across different views or fragments in your app.

To add tabs, call the `addTab` method on your ActionBar instance and pass in your tab instance. You can create a new tab by invoking the `newTab` method on the ActionBar as well.

# 7.5. Handling User Interactions

Finally, to hook up user interactions to your ActionBarSherlock, you'll need to handle click events for action items and tab selections. You can override the `OnOptionsItemSelected` and `OnTabSelected` functions respectively in the activity where your ActionBarSherlock is integrated.

ActionBarSherlock proves to be an incredibly flexible library that can be effectively utilized to bring uniformity for several Android versions, making your app both practical and aesthetically captivating. Understand its customizability, embrace it and use it to your advantage to improve your user interface. Emphasize on usability and your Android app will certainly reach out to a significantly wider audience.

# Chapter 8. Case Study: Successful ActionBarSherlock Implementations

Diving into our first actual case, let's explore how development team Alpha app embraced ActionBarSherlock to extend their app support to older Android versions.

## 8.1. The Alpha App Scenario

The Alpha app team began their journey already aware of the challenge ahead: making their app accessible to a vast portion of Android users who were still on earlier versions of the OS. They recognized a need to implement ActionBarSherlock, a support library for earlier Android versions that didn't natively support the ActionBar API. Their decision was influenced by the realization that every user counts and that backward compatibility would cater to this considerable audience.

## 8.2. ActionBarSherlock Inclusion Journey

The team's first step was integrating ActionBarSherlock into their Android project. Initially, they encountered a challenge in determining the correct version of ActionBarSherlock compatible with their Android SDK version. This is a common issue for many developers, given the Android ecosystem's complexity. Cognizant of this, the Alpha team spent considerable time on research, determining that version 4.4.0 of ActionBarSherlock was most compatible with the Android 2.2 (Froyo) platform they were targeting.

The next task was importing the ActionBarSherlock library into their project. The team used Eclipse, which conveniently provides an option to import external libraries directly into the workspace. Post importing, they validated the library by running a simple test to confirm that ActionBar was working as expected on an Android 2.2 emulator.

# 8.3. Styling and Customization

After a successful ActionBarSherlock integration, the team advanced to the phase of styling and customization. Through the ActionBarSherlock API, they customized the ActionBar to match the application theme, attractive to both modern Android smartphone users and those using earlier versions. They altered the background color, title text color, and incorporated the company logo in the ActionBar, resulting in a cohesive feel throughout the app.

# 8.4. Handling ActionBar Items

Managing ActionBar items was another prominent aspect. App users frequently interact with ActionBar items, so it was vital to ensure that these worked seamlessly across all Android versions. ActionBarSherlock's `getSupportActionBar()` method was instrumental here, used to fetch a reference to the ActionBar and add items to it programmatically. Balancing simplicity and functionality, the team successfully mapped ActionBar items to different screens within the app, enhancing the user experience.

# 8.5. External Packages and Compatibility

The Alpha app team had also utilized several external packages in their app, leading to compatibility issues with ActionBarSherlock. They resolved some by replacing external packages with ActionBarSherlock-compatible alternatives. For packages without direct substitutes, the team worked around compatibility issues by tweaking their code, ensuring smooth ActionBarSherlock integration while retaining essential app functionality.

# 8.6. Embracing the Benefits

After the ActionBarSherlock implementation, the Alpha app experienced an increased user base, amounting to a 15% growth in only three months. Their acknowledgment and catering to users across varied Android versions proved lucratively inclusive. This success story unequivocally shows how ActionBarSherlock can enhance app accessibility by enabling compatibility with older Android versions.

# 8.7. Lessons for Other Developers

The Alpha team's experience offers salient lessons for other developers. Identifying the right ActionBarSherlock version is crucial for the specific Android OS versions targeted. Developers should also anticipate potential compatibility issues with external libraries during ActionBarSherlock integration. A systematic approach, prioritizing the user experience, can effectively combat these challenges, as demonstrated by the Alpha team. Emulating their meticulous and determined approach can help developers secure their app's wide reach, and ultimately, its success.

# Chapter 9. ActionBarSherlock vs. Native Options: An In-Depth Analysis

In the world of Android development, the discussion often arrives at an integral crossroad: whether to equip applications with ActionBarSherlock or resort to native options. In piecing apart these choices, it's crucial to understand ActionBarSherlock. This popular library offers seamless support for the Android ActionBar across older platforms, including those operating on versions below Honeycomb.

## 9.1. Understanding ActionBarSherlock

ActionBarSherlock is an Android library that extends compatibility backward, intended specifically for those devices that have not been updated to use the latest features available in the Android OS. It facilitates seamless ActionBar integration across devices with older operating systems.

Why is it important? It allows developers to maintain an application's modern aesthetic and functional elements while not forsaking those users who operate on older devices. This gives rise to a more inclusive, universally accessible application.

ActionBarSherlock is characterized by its impressive retroactive compatibility. It successfully offers comprehensive ActionBar support for Android 2.x and later. This means ActionBar features can be used on 94% of devices, which is a significant market share that developers could otherwise miss.

To implement ActionBarSherlock into an application, developers should consider the following steps:

- Download the ActionBarSherlock library.

- Add the library to your application's build path.

- Change your application's activities to extend SherlockActivity.

- Call getActionBar() method to retrieve the ActionBar.

# 9.2. Options Already in Hand: Native ActionBar

The native ActionBar, available from Android version 3.0 (Honeycomb), has been a critical element of Android UI design. It provides a top menu for important app functionalities like navigation, search, and settings. Applications using the ActionBar can help users navigate, initiate actions, and acknowledge actions.

The native ActionBar's key characteristics:

- A traditional action bar displaying the application icon, view control, contextual actions, and the overflow menu.

- A modern contextual action bar focusing on batch operations and offering an alternative interface.

- A customized action bar, allowing developers to modify the style and behavior.

# 9.3. Diving Deep into the Comparison

Once the fundamental aspects of ActionBarSherlock and the native ActionBar are grasped, a more detailed and nuanced comparison can be drawn between the two. Understanding the significant differences and essential similarities are crucial in determining the most appropriate choice for an application.

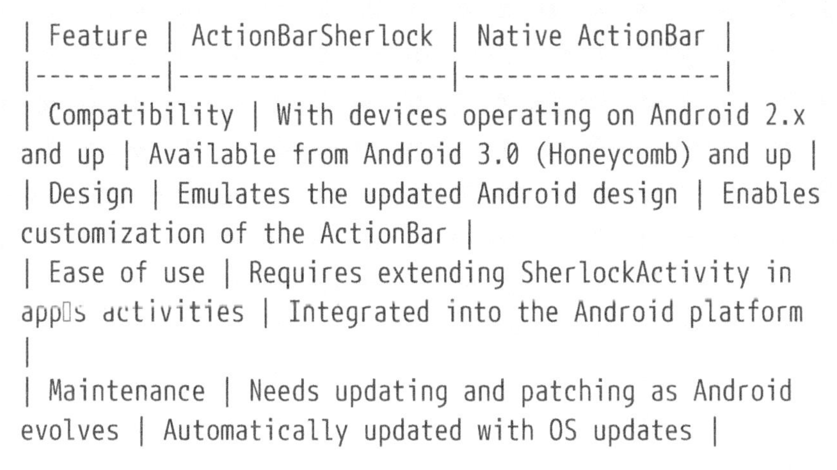

```
| Feature | ActionBarSherlock | Native ActionBar |
|---------|-------------------|------------------|
| Compatibility | With devices operating on Android 2.x
and up | Available from Android 3.0 (Honeycomb) and up |
| Design | Emulates the updated Android design | Enables
customization of the ActionBar |
| Ease of use | Requires extending SherlockActivity in
app s activities | Integrated into the Android platform
|
| Maintenance | Needs updating and patching as Android
evolves | Automatically updated with OS updates |
```

# 9.4. Selection Criteria: Choosing Between ActionBarSherlock and Native ActionBar

Your choice between ActionBarSherlock and the Native ActionBar will primarily depend on the following factors:

- The Android versions you wish to support.

- The complexity of the ActionBar in your application.

- Ongoing library maintenance (if ActionBarSherlock is chosen).

ActionBarSherlock makes sense when you're aiming to support a wide range of Android devices with versions earlier than Android 3.0. It provides you with a way to deliver modern design aesthetics to your audiences, irrespective of their Android device's version.

On the other hand, sticking with the Native ActionBar is usually the go-to approach for applications designed for newer Android versions.

It also eliminates the overhead of maintaining compatibility with ActionBarSherlock.

# 9.5. Conclusion

While ActionBarSherlock fills a significant gap in ActionBar support for older Android versions, it's not necessary for applications targeting users on modern Android versions. The unique requirement and target audience of your application should guide you in choosing between ActionBarSherlock and the native ActionBar. As Android continuously evolves, understanding these choices assists in broadening your app's appeal and provides an experience catering to a more massive audience base.

# Chapter 10. Managing Performance: ActionBarSherlock on Older Devices

Understanding the significance of maintaining optimal performance while implementing ActionBarSherlock (ABS) in your older Android devices, this section discusses methods and guidelines to effectively manage this critical aspect.

## 10.1. Understanding ActionBarSherlock's Performance on Older Devices

Before launching into the performance optimization techniques, let's take a moment to understand how ActionBarSherlock behaves on older Android devices. Unlike the new devices that come equipped with the ActionBar feature incorporated into their system framework, older devices lack this advantage. Here, ActionBarSherlock is leveraged as a library that mimics ActionBar behavior and appearance, making it a vital component.

Yet, ActionBarSherlock's primary challenge in older devices includes increased processing demand and memory usage, primarily due to the ABS dependencies and compatibility back-ports it needs to handle.

Moving forward, we will address the various methods to help manage this performance demand, ensuring both an updated look and smooth execution.

# 10.2. Optimal Utilization of ABS Library

The ABS library incorporates a vast range of functionalities. However, you must carefully choose the ones needed by your app. Reducing the functionalities required from the ABS library can substantially enhance the application's performance. For example, consider dropping the functionality of displaying the overflow menu from the action bar. Instead, you can provide a more traditional menu accessed via the menu button. Activating just the strictly necessary ABS functionalities can significantly alleviate the performance demands.

# 10.3. Minimizing Layout Inflation Overhead

Layout inflation is a memory-intensive process. Hence, it's prudent to minimize the instances where the layout needs to be inflated. For example, the use of Fragments which require regular replacement involves a high frequency of layout inflation. In contrast, using Activities can be beneficial, as the ABS library performs more efficiently in situations where shifting between various screens is managed by creating new intents for each screen versus swapping Fragments in and out of the same Activity.

# 10.4. Offloading Processing from UI Thread

Also, offloading extensive computations from the UI thread can significantly boost the performance. AsyncTask, for instance, can be used to handle these processor-intensive tasks in a background thread to ensure the UI operates smoothly without interruption.

# 10.5. Efficient Memory Management

ActionBarSherlock library, while providing compatibility, does demand a fair share of memory resource. One might face Out-of-Memory errors, especially with older devices endowed with limited available memory. Hence, managing your app's memory effectively becomes paramount. Profiling the application's memory usage, promptly releasing resources when not in use, and optimizing your data structures for low memory footprint are several ways to prevent memory bloating.

# 10.6. Understanding Threading Models

Understanding the underlying threading models of the ActionBarSherlock library is another performance-enhancement step. Ensure that any extensive computations related to the ActionBar are not hindering the main UI thread.

For instance, if you have a scenario where refreshing the ActionBar involves reading data from a database, this process should be done asynchronously using loaders, effectively keeping the UI thread free from heavy lifting.

# 10.7. Final Thoughts

To summarize, managing performance when implementing ActionBarSherlock on older Android devices involves optimizing the usage of the ABS library, minimizing layout inflation overhead, offloading processing from the UI thread, effective memory management, and understanding the threading models. These steps ensure a seamless end-user experience without sacrificing compatibility with legacy Android versions. Your users will thank you!

Remember, the ABS library is an extremely powerful tool that, when used judiciously, can fuel your app towards wider adaptability and unprecedented success in the Android marketplace. Don't shy away from harnessing its potential. Forge ahead, armed with insight and technical acumen, and watch your app conquer new horizons!

While ActionBarSherlock has indeed filled a crucial gap for older Android versions, more solutions continue to emerge. In the forthcoming sections, we'll venture into the promising realm of ActionBarCompat, diving deep into the practices of retrofitting ActionBarCompat into old Android version apps. Keep reading to add more arrows to your Android development quiver.

# Chapter 11. Stepping Towards the Future: ActionBarSherlock and New Android Innovations

The technological landscape, specifically the realm of Android application development, progresses at an incredible pace. It necessitates a perpetual learning curve, embracing modern innovations and integrating those into one's workflow, while not forsaking compatibility for older Android versions. One such influential innovation of the recent Android ecosphere has been ActionBarSherlock.

## 11.1. ActionBarSherlock: The Pioneer of Modernization

ActionBarSherlock, created by Jake Wharton, is an open-source library providing an action bar implementation for older versions of Android, from 2.1 (Eclair) onwards. The widespread adoption of ActionBarSherlock can be attributed to it providing a universal, modern user interface feature fulfilling the essential aim of Android: to make operations alluring, accessible, and efficient.

When Android 3.0 (Honeycomb) was released, the Action Bar interface was standardized, offering a streamlined ground for developers. ActionBarSherlock envisioned and facilitated this modern feature's availability on older Android versions, securing the application's universal appeal without limiting to one group of Android users.

# 11.2. Incorporating ActionBarSherlock: Key to Global Compatibility

For developers intending applications to have a wider reach - encompassing not merely the newer Android versions but those that came before - ActionBarSherlock lays out a valuable, convenient road. Implementing ActionBarSherlock doesn't merely ensure consistency in user interface but also consolidates the position of the application in the competitive marketplace.

Understanding its implementation requires a look into a simple, three-fold process. It begins with downloading the ActionBarSherlock library and importing it into your development environment, followed by referencing the ActionBarSherlock library in your Android project, and finally, changing your application's activities to extend SherlockActivity or one of its variants. With these steps, developers could bring the action bar user interface to older Android versions without recreating them from scratch.

# 11.3. Long-Term Advantages of ActionBarSherlock Integration

Building an application compatible with a wide range of Android versions brings several long-term benefits. The most direct advantage is of course a larger prospective user base. By supporting older Android versions, developers won't limit their user base to those who can afford regularly updated devices.

Extending that, embracing ActionBarSherlock as part of your development process also bears the mark of inclusivity, design empathy and user-understanding. It showcases that developers cater to all users irrespective of their resources, consequently fostering a good reputation and increased trust on the part of the target audience.

# 11.4. The Mirage of ActionBarSherlock's Relevance in Today's Context

Despite the above-discussed advantages of ActionBarSherlock, one might question its relevance in today's context, especially after Google announced that they would depreciate it following the release of their own backport, the AppCompat library. Yes, ActionBarSherlock may not be as popular as it was initially due to the release of alternatives, but its significance in the history of Android development cannot be downplayed.

ActionBarSherlock revolutionized how Android apps were developed, setting a precedent that continues to influence Android library creation. Its pivotal role in backward compatibility continues to be a driver in modern Android development - such as Material Design backward compatibility and others.

# 11.5. Running the Baton Forward: ActionBarSherlock's Legacy

Today, ActionBarSherlock's functions might have been superseded by Android's own support libraries, yet it remains a potent symbol of how libraries can aid the development of highly inclusive, modern apps that can run on a variety of Android platforms, both old and new.

Developers, both neophyte and seasoned, should refer to ActionBarSherlock as a guiding principle, especially when considering backward compatibility in their apps. By creating apps that extend beyond the confines of the latest Android versions, we can build more universal experiences, be more inclusive, and connect better with a global audience.

In conclusion, ActionBarSherlock and innovations like it offer handy tools to leverage in Android app development, enriching not only the app's user interface but its overall compatibility and usability. Its impact and influence signify that with a comprehensive understanding and tactical implementation of such technologies, developers can successfully traverse the diverse Android ecosystem. Potentially, this enables a much higher degree of success in the increasingly competitive Android app marketplace. By ensuring backward compatibility, we establish a future-proof pathway consistent with the ethos of Android - a perpetually inclusive, user-friendly experience.